PRAYING
WITH
POWER

PRAYING WITH POWER

Rex Humbard

abridged from
"THE PRAYER KEY"
Copyright 1974
by The Rex Humbard Ministry
Akron, Ohio

© 1975 by New Hope Press
ISBN: 0-8010-4140-6

TABLE OF CONTENTS

Chapter I

PRAYER IS POTENT

"Ask, and it shall be given you; seek, and ye shall find; knock, and it shall be opened unto you: For every one that asketh receiveth; and he that seeketh findeth; and to him that knocketh it shall be opened"

(Matthew 7:7, 8).

Early in life God taught me the power of prayer. Some of the first sounds I remember from childhood were those of Mom and Dad praying. Although my parents were both preachers, I had to learn firsthand how potent prayer really is. One of the most forceful lessons I learned during those times was when God used a total stranger to feed our family.

The Humbard family was preaching and singing on the radio in Hot Springs, Arkansas, and struggling to build a little church for the glory of God. I was about thirteen years old at the time and sang on the radio every day with the rest of the family. Our house seemed to always be full of evangelists, missionaries, and traveling preachers coming through our community. Although we barely had enough to eat, my folks always had enough to share. One Saturday evening a Christian lady who had been staying with us told Mom, "Mrs. Humbard, we have run out of food. There is absolutely nothing to feed the family tomorrow." Mom listened and then said, "Mrs. Childs, you just think of what you would like to cook, go in and put the pots and pans on the stove just like you have the food. God

5

will fill the pots." Then Mom went in the bedroom and started praying.

Early Sunday morning we were awakened by a knock on the front door. When Dad answered he saw a stranger standing there shuffling from one foot to the other. He said, "Brother Humbard, I've been listening to your kids sing on the radio every day. Well, this morning about four o'clock, I woke up and something inside me said, "Take some groceries to them kids you've been hearin'." At first I argued thinking that I would probably insult you-all if I brought you some food. Yet, the more I argued, the more I knew I had to do it. Well, here I am and I have a truckload of groceries for you out here, if it won't make you mad."

Such a load of groceries I have never seen. The farmer had dug up a pile of potatoes, almost cleaned out his smokehouse for meat, and brought about every kind of vegetable you could imagine. Needless to say, the Humbards had a feast that day and I learned an important lesson about the potency of prayer.

Novelist Kathleen Norris says, "I base my whole life on prayer. A hundred times a day my thoughts go to the One human life that so supremely influenced the world and I renew my faith in my relationship with the Savior of mankind. I have silently prayed during great battles, during crises in the nursery, at glittering dinner tables, and as a speaker on flag-draped platforms. Gradually the miracle has been forced on me that no prayer goes unanswered. It may be answered by seeming disappointment, even humiliation. It often is answered in a totally unexpected way, or when it has been forgotten even by the suppliant. The insufferable has disappeared, the unbearable has become precious and right, the heartbreak has become heart's-ease."

Many people use prayer as a fire escape or an

S.O.S. Tragically they view prayer as the last resort when all hope is gone. They are like the lady who, hearing the doctor say she should pray for her ill husband, gasped, "Has it come to that?" Those who view prayer as a spare tire to be used only in emergencies are failing to know what a dynamic and exciting life they can have in Christ. Prayer can and should be as normal as breathing in and out. When it becomes a vital part of our lives, we will be more free of tensions that tear much of mankind and we will be full of faith that can indeed make our life on this earth vibrant.

Often overlooked in the life of our Lord was the part prayer played. Much of His earthly time was spent in communication with His heavenly Father. In fact, His disciples seemed to know that the dynamics of Christ's earthly life were wrapped up in His prayer time. Note they requested Christ to "Teach us how to pray." They did not ask Him to teach them how to perform miracles, heal the sick, or raise the dead. They understood these expressions of power came from the living relationship Jesus had with His Father. It was the same type of relationship they wanted in their lives and ministries. And, that relationship is available to believers today.

Jesus spoke often and clearly about the power of prayer. One day, late in His earthly life, Christ said, "Verily, verily, I say unto you, He that believeth on me, the works that I do shall he do also; and greater works than these shall he do; because I go unto my Father. And whatsoever ye shall ask in my name, that will I do, that the Father may be glorified in the Son" (John 14:12, 13). Our Lord has actually promised each one of us a dynamic life and ministry through prayer.

One might ask, "What is greater than healing the sick or raising the dead?" Jesus did all of these.

Yet, in our generation we have the privilege of reaching the masses with the message of Christ through television, a work Christ could not accomplish in His day. Indeed that prophecy of our Lord has been fulfilled and today we are involved in the greatest work of all, that of reaching millions of souls for our Savior. And, this ministry did not just happen. Rather, it came about because God's children everywhere prayed. These pray-ers have multiplied their witness around the world just as Jesus said they would. Such is the power of prayer.

Staggering as it is to realize, Christ has placed within our hands the most potent power in the universe. One day Jesus said, "Verily I say unto you, Whatsoever ye shall bind on earth shall be bound in heaven: and whatsoever ye shall loose on earth shall be loosed in heaven. Again I say unto you, That if two of you shall agree on earth as touching any thing that they shall ask, it shall be done for them of my Father which is in heaven" (Matthew 18:18, 19). The disciples understood the power of prayer. They knew that while prayer to most people was a form, to Christ it was a force. They had seen Him go into prayer in one mood and come out in another. They saw things changed because of His prayer and knew how much He prayed. No wonder they pleaded, "Lord, teach us to pray."

It is because I deeply feel prayer is the most powerful force in the universe that I share this prayer book with you. When I started into television over twenty years ago, people began to write us for prayer. We soon began a 24-hour prayer group and our prayer ministry has grown and grown. We have received thousands of letters testifying how the prayers we shared together have changed lives and brought meaning to millions. Our prayer time has grown until now it is the most powerful part of our whole ministry. Through prayer we can and will effect change in the life of our world.

Not long ago the prominent Judge, Harold R. Medina, said, "The first step toward spiritual strength is taken when each of us comes to realize that we cannot accomplish really worthwhile things in life all by ourselves. When we turn to the true source for strength and guidance, when prayer becomes a habit, when we tell God not once but many times a day that we love Him and want Him close to us, we are on our way. I have lived a full, exciting life as a lawyer and as a judge fighting for what I thought was right. In every crisis I turned to God for help and I never called for help in vain."

Prayer is the key to moving heaven and earth for God. We have the thrilling role of cooperating with God in the redemptive process through prayer. And, this is exciting. But, prayer is even more than this. It is also a power to help us with the problems of life we face every day. Through prayer we can live a vital and exciting life of faith known only by those who have walked this path before us. Too often we strain and struggle through life, seeming to lose more than we win. I deeply believe God has a victorious life of faith for us and we can find that life through communion with Him. I agree with the songwriter:

> "Oh, what peace we often forfeit,
>   Oh, what needless pain we bear,
> All because we do not carry
>   Ev'rything to God in prayer!"

Chapter II

PRIVILEGES OF PRAYER

"And when thou prayest, thou shalt not be as the hypocrites are: for they love to pray standing in the synagogues and in the corners of the streets, that they may be seen of men. Verily I say unto you, They have their reward"

(Matthew 6:5).

Prayer has always played an important part in the lives of many famous men. President James Garfield was a popular lay preacher who made no secret of his strong belief in the power of prayer. Statesman Dag Hammarskjold often spoke of his dependence on divine direction through prayer. And, perhaps the most-loved and best-known of all United States presidents was Abraham Lincoln. He talked much about the place of prayer in his life.

During the trying hours of the Civil War Lincoln leaned heavily on divine direction. Of those hours he wrote, "I have had so many evidences of His direction, so many instances of time when I have been controlled by some other power than my own will, that I cannot doubt that this power comes from God. I frequently see my way clear to a decision when I am conscious that I have not sufficient facts on which to found it. I am satisfied that, when the Almighty wants me to do, or not to do, a particular thing, He finds a way of letting me know. I talk to God and when I do my mind seems relieved and a way is suggested."

While most people would agree that prayer is a good thing and does work, still there is much confusion about what prayer actually is and how it works. Most people's idea of prayer is far too narrow. To some prayer is the closed eye, the bended knee, the raised hand. They think of it as a specific activity confined to a certain time and place. This may be part of prayer but it is not all there is to prayer. Prayer encompasses all of life. It moves beyond words to the sincere desire of the heart. One's very life style is a prayer.

Not long ago I went through a great crisis in my ministry. During that time I spent eight days fasting and praying about direction in my ministry. From that experience I felt new strength and power come into my life. That was a special time for a special purpose. There are other times when prayer is just as real but not as intense. Our whole lives are prayers. I know all I want to do in life is win more souls for Christ. Therefore, everything I do is for that purpose. We have our board of trustees meeting at the church and that is a form of prayer for our ministry. Whatever we do, even in the secular world, if it is for the single purpose of serving Christ and winning souls, then that is prayer. Prayer is actually living in faith, believing you are a child of God and having the desire to keep the commandments of the Lord and do His work. Only when we understand this concept of prayer can we truly "pray without ceasing."

There are four basic attitudes in prayer and these are outlined carefully by the Apostle Paul to young Timothy. Paul says, "I exhort therefore, that, first of all, supplications, prayers, intercessions, and giving of thanks, be made for all men; For kings, and for all that are in authority; that we may lead a quiet and peaceable life in all godliness and honesty" (I Timothy 2:1, 2).

11

Supplication Is Asking

Joseph Scriven captured the plight of many people in the song, "What a Friend." In one verse he laments, "Oh, what peace we often forfeit, Oh, what needless pain we bear, All because we do not carry Ev'rything to God in prayer!" Tragically, many shuffle through life half living because they have not learned God wishes them to ask Him for various blessings during their earthly life. James noted, "Ye lust, and have not: ye kill, and desire to have, and cannot obtain: ye fight and war, yet ye have not, because ye ask not" (James 4:2). Jesus frankly told us the giving nature of God when He said, "Fear not, little flock; for it is your Father's good pleasure to give you the kingdom" (Luke 12:32).

Part of prayer is asking. Paul tells young Timothy not to be slack in asking God. This is supplication. God's Word clearly encourages us to not be hesitant about the privilege of asking in prayer, "Let us therefore come boldly unto the throne of grace, that we may obtain mercy, and find grace to help in time of need" (Hebrews 4:16).

Dr. Walter H. Judd, missionary and congressman, learned the privilege of asking during the tense days in China when he wondered if he would survive the revolution. He wrote, "When I went to China in 1925 as a medical missionary, I had in my heart this promise of Christ; '. . . lo, I am with you alway even unto the end of the world . . .' (Matthew 28:20).

"I was afraid maybe that it wouldn't be true, but it is. In 1930, during eight months when I was in a polite sort of captivity, nobody in the city took off his clothes at night because the Communists might arrive at his door. I had quinine, money, and a flashlight always near at hand, in case I had to get away at a moment's notice. I would wake up every morning wondering what that day would bring forth, and would pray this simple prayer: 'O Master, let me walk with Thee in lowly paths of service free. Tell me Thy secret!'

"There would come into my spirit something that supported and helped steady me, gave me confidence and assurance during the day. I can't explain it. I can't explain how some of the food I ate tonight for supper becomes brain, some blood, some bone, but I haven't stopped eating just because I can't explain it! In the same way, I cannot explain this. It is not in the realm of explanation yet, or of logical proof. It is in the realm of demonstration; prayer works."

Lest we think that prayer is merely a purchase order to get what we want in life, Paul moves on to tell young Timothy of a deeper dimension. He explains that effective prayer moves beyond the level of asking to that of communion. This is what the second part of his instructions indicates.

Communion With The Creator

James tells his readers, "Ye ask and receive not, because ye ask amiss, that ye may consume it upon your lusts" (James 4:3). Therefore, if a person is to be an effective pray-er he must have a living relationship with the Master so he might know what is the will of the Father. Prayer is that relationship of communion where the two wills, God's and man's, blend into one. Christ's dramatic prayer in the garden was that of bending His earthly will to the Father's heavenly will. This is only done through communion with God.

When Jesus taught His disciples to pray, He gave a simple formula we today identify as "The Lord's

13

Prayer." Although the prayer has only 66 words and requires but twenty seconds to say, yet its power has long been recognized by believers. And, that potent prayer starts with "Our Father." Here Christ sets the mood for effective communication with God. We are to address Him on a personal basis. "ABBA" in Aramaic, Jesus' mother tongue, could best be translated as "Papa."

Ernest O. Hauser noted, "There is no trace of the awe with which a fearful people might approach its sovereign lord. We count on God's benevolence. Between supplicant and listener a relationship of trust is established. We have come as children, to discuss family matters. By authorizing us to approach God in this way, Christ gives us the benefit of His own intimate relationship with the Father."

Those who limit their prayers to mere purchase orders, to be rubber stamped and supplied by God, will continue to wonder why their prayers are not answered. However, when one moves into the deeper dimension of communion with God, He begins to be more selective in His requests, wishing only that they conform to the will of the Master. We continue to ask, but through fellowship; we ask according to His will and are thrilled when we see the many mysterious ways these requests are answered by a loving Christ.

While some are stymied in their prayer life by asking amiss, there are others who give up too easily. Therefore, Paul encourages Timothy to consider still another facet of prayer; that of intercession. Intercession could best be defined as the patient pleading for something in the face of discouragement and seeming despair. And, there are times in our lives when we must be involved in this ministry of intercession.

Patient Pleadings

Many fail to understand the stranglehold satan has on this world. Therefore, they often misunderstand the purpose of intercession. They often view God as a reluctant Giver who has to be begged, cajoled, maybe even threatened, before He finally gives something to His children. Such a distorted view of God breeds discontent and resentment, rather than love and trust. It must be understood that intercession is necessary because satan is the god of this world, not because our Father is reluctant to give. This premise is made crystal clear in the dramatic life of Daniel.

After God had given Daniel the troubling vision of the future, Daniel sought long for its meaning. He said, "In those days I Daniel was mourning three full weeks. I ate no pleasant bread, neither came flesh nor wine in my mouth, neither did I anoint myself at all, till three whole weeks were fulfilled" (Daniel 10:2, 3). During this time he had sought God for an answer, but it seemed his prayers were not even being heard. Daniel was deeply disturbed and wondered why God would not answer.

Finally, a dramatic encounter explained the problem. Daniel had a visitor from the heavenly realm who explained, ". . . Fear not, Daniel: for from the first day that thou didst set thine heart to understand, and to chasten thyself before thy God, thy words were heard, and I am come for thy words. But the prince of the kingdom of Persia withstood me one and twenty days: but, lo, Michael, one of the chief princes, came to help me; and I remained there with the kings of Persia. Now I am come to make thee understand what shall befall thy people in the latter days: for yet the vision is for many days" (Daniel 10:12-14).

Ever since man fell in the Garden, this earth has

15

been locked in the vise of the evil one. Paul reminded us, "For we wrestle not against flesh and blood, but against principalities, against powers, against the rulers of the darkness of this world, against spiritual wickedness in high places" (Ephesians 6:12). We are involved in a mortal struggle with satan for the souls of men. Therefore, intercession, that patient pleading for their souls, is part of our prayer life.

To emphasize the importance of intercession Jesus said, ". . . Which of you shall have a friend, and shall go unto him at midnight, and say unto him, Friend, lend me three loaves; For a friend of mine in his journey is come to me, and I have nothing to set before him? And he from within shall answer and say, Trouble me not: the door is now shut, and my children are with me in bed; I cannot rise and give thee. I say unto you, Though he will not rise and give him, because he is his friend, yet because of his importunity he will rise and give him as many as he needeth" (Luke 11:5-8). Jesus went on to add, ". . . Ask, and it shall be given you; seek, and ye shall find; knock, and it shall be opened unto you" (Luke 11:9).

When we recognize Jesus clearly taught the necessity of intercession, and God's Word explains that this world is locked in darkness until the time Christ returns, then we can know the necessity and power of intercession. If we ask and keep on asking, God will answer. We must be given to intercession if we are to wrestle souls from the clutches of satan.

Giving Of Thanks

The fourth facet of effective praying is that of giving thanks. This is a leap of faith where we accept as already accomplished what we have prayed for. Praise also keeps us from becoming egocentric in our spiritual lives. Through it we recognize that God alone is the answer to our prayers. While we may be involved in the answer, still it is He who gives the strength, wisdom, and means to accomplish what we have prayed might be done. Praise moves us from a self-centered existence to a Christ-centered one.

Giving thanks is too often a lost art of the believer. Yet, God's Word clearly commands, "By him therefore let us offer the sacrifice of praise to God continually, that is, the fruit of our lips giving thanks to his name" (Hebrews 13:15). We give thanks because it is commanded, it glorifies God, and it is good for us. The wise believer will make praise part of his everyday spiritual life.

First Of All

Some time ago a preacher friend told me of an encounter he had with another Christian about a certain religious leader his friend was criticizing. The pastor gently rebuked the brother for the criticism by asking, "Have you ever prayed for this man?" The man replied, "No," and to this the wise pastor suggested, "God's Word says, '. . . first of all, supplications, prayers, intercessions, and giving of thanks, be made for all men' (I Timothy 2:1). Sir, only after we have prayed for that person are we then permitted to criticize." How wise this lesson. If we would put our priorities in proper place then our comments about others would be tempered by Christ-like concern. What a revival of love the church would have if we followed the Lord's commandments here!

Prayer is a privilege and a responsibility. I trust we rise to the challenge and explore its full dimensions of power. Only then will we know the revival the world seeks. I have found fasting to be a practical way in which to move toward more effective praying.

Chapter III

FASTING FOR ADDED POWER

"Moreover when ye fast, be not, as the hypocrites, of a sad countenance: for they disfigure their faces, that they may appear unto men to fast. Verily I say unto you, They have their reward"

(Matthew 6:16).

"Today is a very special day in my life," the letter began. "One year ago today," it continued, "I accepted Christ. I have to praise God for the whole past year, but I also want you and everyone on your staff to know that without you people, I would have probably been running the same way that I was. I was once a glory-hound, trying to show the world how to play basketball. I'm eighteen years old and a new person.

"Thirteen months ago, I never even thought I would see the inside of a Bible. I was hung up on modern music, pornography, and ego. Now, I've accepted Christ and I'm really happy. I attend all of your TV rallies in the area. Again, I want to thank everyone that makes your ministry work, and I am praying to God that you are as successful with others as you have been with me."

Soon after receiving this letter another viewer wrote me to say, "For forty-four years I was deep in sin, drinking, and gambling. I went through three marriages, lost my business, money, wife, and everything I had. I was really on the bottom and had to move in with my mother. She prayed for me for years. Every Sunday morning she put on Channel 5, Cathedral of Tomorrow.

"One Sunday you talked about the son that came back to his father. That sermon really got to me. Right then I asked the Lord to forgive me of all my sins, and He delivered me from drink and gambling; and it has stayed that way. Would you believe, I am going to a Four Square church now and singing in the choir? When the Lord does a job, He really does it well. I'm glad the Lord loved me even when I was in sin, and that He didn't give up on me. Rex, you never know when something you say might mean everything to someone. Keep up the good work till Jesus comes."

Testimonies like these thrill the heart. And, because so many come in to our office each week, some might think souls are saved with very little effort. This is far from the truth. Every letter and word of testimony we receive is the result of millions of prayers and much fasting over this ministry. This is why we have placed such an importance on the ministry of prayer.

One day Jesus healed a boy driven by evil forces within himself. The child's father explained to Jesus, "Lord, have mercy on my son: for he is lunatick, and sore vexed: for ofttimes he falleth into the fire, and oft into the water. And I brought him to thy disciples, and they could not cure him" (Matthew 17:15, 16). After the Master had delivered the child, Christ's disciples asked, ". . . Why could not we cast him out?" (Matthew 17:19). To this Jesus replied, "Howbeit this kind goeth not out but by prayer and fasting" (Matthew 17:21).

When we come up against the full forces of evil, we have a desperate struggle on our hands. Satan does not relinquish control of his bound ones easily. This is especially true when a person has been a slave to sin for many years. For this reason Jesus gave us the secret to added strength, that of fasting in prayer.

Bound In The Body

Our souls are bound in the human body. Most often we give more attention to the care of our bodies than those needs of the soul. We are driven by powers of the body, such as hunger and thirst. Of course there is nothing wrong with these drives but the man who always is a slave to them is never really free. The purpose of fasting is to give proper attention to the needs of the soul rather than relenting to the drives of the body. Fasting breaks the surly bonds of our carnal man.

Fasting deprives this outward body. It is part of keeping our bodies under subjection. Paul admonishes, "I beseech you therefore, brethren, by the mercies of God, that ye present your bodies a living sacrifice, holy, acceptable unto God, which is your reasonable service. And be not conformed to this world: but be ye transformed by the renewing of your mind, that ye may prove what is that good, and acceptable, and perfect, will of God" (Romans 12:1, 2).

Fasting helps us do these two things—to present our bodies and to let our minds be transformed by Christ.

False Fast

Fasting moves us from selfishness to service. Isaiah grappled with the difference between a real and counterfeit fast. During his day there were those who went through the motions of fasting as a performance rather than as a desire to move with the will of God. He said, "Behold, ye fast for strife and debate, and to smite with the fist of wickedness . . ." (Isaiah 58:4). The great prophet then moves on to quote God, "Is not this the fast that I have chosen? to loose the bands of wickedness, to undo the heavy burdens, and to let the oppressed go free, and that ye break every yoke? Is it not to deal thy bread to the hungry, and that thou bring the poor that are cast out to thy house? when thou seest the naked, that thou cover him; and that thou hide not thyself from thine own flesh?" (Isaiah 58:6, 7).

When we fast and pray God shares with us His very heart's desire. We truly become broken with the things that break the heart of God. This deep communion we share with Him washes pretension from our eyes until we can more clearly discern spiritual matters. For this reason the ones who really want to make an impact for the gospel with their lives will be involved in the meaningful ministry of fasting.

Exciting Results

While we wish to outline clearly the sacrifice of service, we are also quick to point out the added dimension of power that fasting brings to a life. The one who has followed Christ in this school of discipline is more effective in his life and more fruitful in his ministry. In the congregation at the Cathedral of Tomorrow, we have seen this premise work time after time. The Nathan Jones family is a vivid example of the tremendous results of praying people.

Seventeen members of the three-generation Jones family have come to know Christ through the prayers of Mr. and Mrs. Nathan Jones. Of this group two were alcoholics, two were hospitalized after suicide attempts, one had planned to kill himself and found Christ just in time. Another had spent twenty-one months in psychotherapy, one had been committed to the psychiatric ward, several had shattered marriages and one was on drugs. However, God saved all and today they are living powerful Christian lives of happiness and service. The Jones family are quick to testify to the power of prayer with fasting and how Christ can change all. Mrs. Jones said, "Eleven years ago we, as a family, were 'a ship of fools' on our way to hell. All has changed now."

The power of fasting was again brought home to me when I recently sought God for eight days. During that time he gave clear direction and I let go of a lot of things that kept me from doing the greatest thing of all, winning souls. I feel my life has been deepened and my ministry strengthened because of this fasting. I remember another crisis in my life when fasting with prayer saved the life of our son.

Back in 1949 we had been traveling and preaching all over America. Rex Jr. was but a boy and suddenly in Detroit he got very ill. We took him to the doctor and X-rays revealed he had a collapsed lung. The doctor was very concerned that the other lung would become infected and if this happened it would kill him. He recommended we take him to a warmer climate and let him get plenty of rest.

We took a month off from our revival meetings and went to Fort Worth, Texas. Oral Roberts had just held a revival meeting there. We had known Oral for several years, but had never been in one of his meetings. In Fort Worth we heard he was going to be in Mobile, Alabama, so we decided to go on down there.

At that particular time I was seeking the Lord for not only Rex's healing, but also for a new dimension in my ministry. I had fasted for 17 days and attended each service, morning and night. The very first night of the meeting we were the first in line when Oral prayed for people. God touched Rex Jr. and after the meeting we took him back to the doctor. He had been healed and no damage had been done to the lungs.

God answered our prayers and healed our son because we were seeking Christ with all our hearts. Many make the mistake of seeking the healing, rather than the Healer. And, these people are always disappointed. When we sincerely seek Christ in fasting and prayer, He always meets us with His divine touch. Fasting is a denial of self, total devotion to Christ, and a discipline of the body.

Fasting is very much part of an effective prayer life. However, there is another dimension to prayer that we often overlook. That is giving. While it is possible to give without praying, it is never possible to really pray without giving.

Chapter IV

GIVING OPENS HEAVEN

"But this I say, He which soweth sparingly shall reap also sparingly; and he which soweth bountifully shall reap also bountifully. Every man according as he purposeth in his heart, so let him give; not grudgingly, or of necessity: for God loveth a cheerful giver"

(II Corinthians 9:6, 7).

One of the most frequent charges made against the church is, "All they ever want is your money." Tragically, some people blinded by this hoax of the devil really believe this and lock up their lives in loneliness and selfishness. While the church might suffer some from lack of funds, it is really the person who withholds that is kept from great blessing.

Whenever I see the gaudy gambling houses of Las Vegas or Reno, I am made vividly aware of how deceptive this hoax of satan really is. There people stand for hours pulling handles on slot machines, throwing dice on tables, or trying their luck at cards, until most often they lose all they have. But, when one loses all his money in these establishments, he is of no further use to them and they discard him. If he were sick, they would not visit him. They would not preach his funeral or comfort his family. They care nothing for his eternal soul. Yet, these very people charge that the church is after people's money. What a tragic web of deception satan has been able to weave!

No doubt it is because so many blessings become

ours when we learn to give, that satan has sought to deceive so many. From the very beginning of God's Word the premise of giving and sharing has been taught. God early promises, "Bring ye all the tithes into the storehouse, that there may be meat in mine house, and prove me now herewith, saith the Lord of hosts, if I will not open you the windows of heaven, and pour you out a blessing, that there shall not be room enough to receive it. And I will rebuke the devourer for your sakes, and he shall not destroy the fruits of your ground; neither shall your vine cast her fruit before the time in the field, saith the Lord of hosts" (Malachi 3:10, 11).

Clearly the promise of receiving is tied closely to the premise of giving. Haggai talked about the selfishness of God's people saying, "Ye have sown much, and bring in little; ye eat, but ye have not enough; ye drink, but ye are not filled with drink; ye clothe you, but there is none warm; and he that earneth wages earneth wages to put it into a bag with holes. Thus saith the Lord of hosts; Consider your ways" (Haggai 1:6, 7). Satan would like for us to shut up our giving and thus close off our receiving. Mr. and Mrs. Art DuBro learned this lesson of giving and receiving in the early days of their Christian lives.

The DuBros own and operate a small business and recently shared with me what God had taught them about giving. "Rex, we have been with you about three years now. You helped us put Christ first in our lives, and if we had not turned on our television set one Sunday morning and just happened to hear you, we might still be searching for the truth.

"We started out in a small business five years ago on nothing except debts—no capital, no money for equipment—only hope and hard work. A year or two later (we hadn't found Christ yet) we began to make some progress.

"We started, once we were saved and were regular viewers of your program, trying to send you a little money each month, usually about $20.00, sometimes not even that.

"Our business naturally grew some, but we had no new cars or trucks—no new home. When we needed things, if we did, God provided them. We still had no large bank account. Sometimes on Sunday, when we would sit down to write your check, it left nothing in our account at all.

"But! When we read in our paper one day, about the end of March, of your trouble, our hearts were troubled deeply. I told my husband, 'We'll have to help Rex. I'm sending $100, and, from here on, ten percent of our income, whatever it is, and more if we can.' It frightened me a little because I knew how slim our account was and how big our debts. But we felt God would supply our needs. Well, since we sent the first $100, there has not been a single week that we have not been able to send anywhere from $50 to $100 per week—not per month. We have doubled our business from last year. We are sending ten to twenty times the amount we were sending, and there is never a time after we send your check on Sunday, that God does not 'throw it right back in the nest'—and more— usually by the end of the next day.

"We still do not have wealth as some would see it. As you said today, some would call us fools. But, thank God, we know better.

"I hope we can attend the next conference. We give God all praise and all the glory. We give expecting nothing. We give to God because we love Him and because we love you and believe in what you're doing. Your services have helped us find God as we know they have so many others, and we

27

hope, with God's help, we can send more and more, and we witness for God every chance we get."

There is an eternal law of God concerning giving. Paul tells of this in II Corinthians, "But this I say, He which soweth sparingly shall reap also sparingly; and he which soweth bountifully shall reap also bountifully" (II Corinthians 9:6). Paul moves on in this thought by declaring, "Every man according as he purposeth in his heart, so let him give; not grudgingly, or of necessity: for God loveth a cheerful giver. And God is able to make all grace abound toward you; that ye, always having all sufficiency in all things, may abound to every good work" (II Corinthians 9:7, 8).

Not long ago a friend shared a lesson he learned about giving. He said, "My wife and I went to church all our lives and we always hoped we would have a home in Heaven, but were never sure. Nineteen years ago we listened to Rex on the radio and this started a change in our lives. We both accepted the Lord as our personal Savior and we knew we were saved and born again. At first we could not understand why our self-righteousness and the good things we had done were not enough, but the Lord reminded me in His Word they were as filthy rags and for my glory only.

"My health at this time was very poor. Doctors were not able to help me. I had a nervous condition, ulcers, sinus condition, and arthritis. After I was saved all these things began to leave as I was obedient to what I read in the Bible. After about two years the eye glasses I wore for about ten years were gone. The doctor said they were not needed any more. Now, nineteen years later at 61 years of age, my doctor says I have perfect health, which is greater than all the wealth in the world. It came about by the Lord's influence to give my money, my time, and prayers.

"At the beginning when I heard and read about tithing, it was hard to give ten percent. When I made up my mind to stick with it, then things started to improve. I began to have more left over than I had before and other blessings were added to my life and family. So, I increased my tithes as the Bible says to give as thou hast prospered.

"After I was saved, I took the Lord into my business as a partner. Some people say religion and business don't mix, but I found out it makes the best business. My business began to prosper where others failed. I turned all the worries and troubles over to the Lord. Even people in my employ were saved and their lives changed for the better. The customers are always satisfied.

"I don't understand how the Lord does it—when you give and go the extra miles, you get more in return.

"I took the Lord as a partner in my life and home and this made harmony in the home between me and my wife and a big improvement between me and my six children because we talked things over and had better communication.

"I mortgaged my home and gave it to help build the Cathedral of Tomorrow where I have seen thousands of people saved and helped. I also gave all my savings and the Lord returned it double in two years' time. The Lord said to me if I would do this, He would take care of me and my family and He has. None of us has ever been in the hospital in the last nineteen years.

"My own six children grew up in Sunday school at the Cathedral of Tomorrow and never learned to smoke or drink. Three of them have been married in the Cathedral and we have three at home. This takes a heavy load off of parents when the children have this kind of teaching.

"I give some time in prayer every day for Cathedral needs, Cathedral TV prayer requests, out-of-town rallies and my family and people I meet that have a need for the Lord. This is on a card I carry with me all the time, and I am blessed by seeing prayers answered often for these needs.

"My wife and I give of our time in the Sunday school and personal counseling at the Cathedral. I also do visitation in the home and hospital and still have time to run a business, play golf, go to Florida for three weeks in January, and do things with my family. Every year I have extra money from the business after taxes.

"The Lord's work needs it more than I do, so I give this extra money instead of putting it in the bank at interest because the Lord pays back principal and interest tenfold in peace of mind and health and many other blessings. Anyway, I don't need this extra because the Lord supplies all of my needs and not my wants so I make good use of everything I own. The Lord uses it and I use it.

"If we don't give anything to God, or do anything for God, we cannot expect to receive anything except our free gift of Salvation, because God measures to us with the same measure as we give.

"After nineteen years I still have more left and good health and peace of mind plus an abundant life ahead because Jesus came into my life."

Wise stewards of God realize their privilege and responsibility in giving. In prayer we give of our time, talent, and tithe. Many times God helps us be the answers to our own prayers by providing the means whereby men may find Christ. It is still true, "The liberal soul shall be made fat: and he that watereth shall be watered also himself" (Proverbs 11:25).

When I announced that I wanted to build the Cathedral of Tomorrow, I showed our television audience a picture of the proposed building. The next week I received an envelope from a little grandmother in West Virginia. She had taken a quarter and carefully sewn it to a card, placed it in the envelope and mailed it to me saying, "I want to help." Of all the mail I have received, I suppose that quarter has meant more to me and was more encouraging. The reason is that I knew this quarter was very precious to that little grandmother. She didn't want it to get lost so she carefully sewed it to a card. She wanted that money in God's work. I believe God will reward her for her gift just as much as he rewards the ones who give the most.

Satan would like to deceive us into not opening our heart of giving to this ministry of winning the lost world. If he causes us to shut off this source of help, then he can do much to destroy the work of God and change believers from generous and loving people into selfish and merciless people. The Apostle John frankly warns, "But whoso hath this world's good, and seeth his brother have need, and shutteth up his bowels of compassion from him, how dwelleth the love of God in him?" (I John 3:17). Today the world has needs greater than any time in human history. I deeply believe we must rise to the challenge.

I shall never forget when the impact of the television ministry really hit me. In the winter of 1952 we held a tent revival in Akron and planned to establish our headquarters here. We wanted to start programs on several area radio stations. During this time someone mentioned to me that there were more people living and breathing in our generation than have lived and died since Adam. The thought gripped my heart as nothing had before. I would wake up in the middle of the night with this thought haunting me. We were having 6,000 in the tent meeting each night but this was a drop in the bucket to what God wanted us to do. Right then I dedicated myself to a ministry of reaching the world for Christ through television. For twenty years we have been faithful to this calling and today the burden weighs even heavier on us to continue this ministry. We all must give so that the world can live.

Chapter V

PROBLEMS IN PRAYER

*"Now we know that God heareth not sinners:
but if any man be a worshipper of God, and doeth
his will, him he heareth"*

(John 9:31).

Several years ago I heard about an old lady who
lived far back in the hills, who heard about but did
not believe in the telephone. Friends had told her
of this marvelous invention, but she could not believe such a thing really existed. She wrote letters
to friends in town and patiently waited for their
answers. She sent her husband driving through the
night for the veterinarian. For her the telephone did
not exist.

Then one day this woman visited the city. There,
for the first time, she saw a phone and learned how
it worked. She immediately ordered one installed at
her farm and began to enjoy the benefits of this
form of communication. A lot of people look at
prayer as that lady saw the phone. For them it
doesn't exist, because they have never seen its effect
in their own lives. Yet, if they would ever really
try it, using the pattern Christ gave, they would find
a new and vital link with the Creator.

There are others who have been praying and
praying and still feel they are getting nowhere.
They wrongly conclude that prayer doesn't work.
However, they probably have been suffering with a
short circuit in their prayer system that breaks the
communication down. If the prayer lines are tan-
gled or down, then communication will be unclear

or totally broken. And, God's Word talks much about things that will destroy our life of prayer.

Prayer Only Works For Those Whose Hearts Are Pure

Prayer is a privilege reserved for the believer. Jesus clearly said, "Now we know that God heareth not sinners: but if any man be a worshipper of God, and doeth his will, him he heareth" (John 9:31). Therefore, if prayer is to work, then the lines of communication have to be first set up by coming to Christ and asking Him to forgive our sins. The sinner's cry is the only prayer the Lord hears from them. The privilege of daily communication is for those who love Jesus.

Many people would like the privilege of prayer without purification of soul. One day Jesus asked a very sick man a sobering question, "Wilt thou be made whole?" The ready answer would seem to be "yes." However, I have found out that many people do not really want to be released from their sin. They only want relief from the pressure it brings. An alcoholic woman had prayed for years that she would get over her problem. Finally, her spiritual advisor helped her understand that she wasn't really wanting to be made whole, only sober. When she submitted her life totally to Christ, was freed of the resentments she harbored, then she was also set free from her drinking. Prayers of people who refuse to be cleansed of their sins will always go unanswered because the lines are down.

There are times in the hearts of those who know Christ when resentments and sins slip in. When this happens believers have problems in prayer. God's Word clearly says, "If I regard iniquity in my heart, the Lord will not hear me" (Psalm 66:18). So, if our prayers are being blocked, it might be good to check our heart to make sure we have sought forgiveness for things we have done. We cannot ignore the tiny hurts we cause people, the thoughtless acts of unkindness, or the disregard we may have for others. These things rise up and block the paths of our prayers.

Psychologists have helped us understand there are four basic destructive emotions that keep us from effective living. They are: fear, guilt, inferiority, and hatred. Long before psychologists discovered these, Jesus spoke clearly of all four and dealt with them at Calvary. Through Christ our fears and guilt are gone. We recognize that we now are sons of the King and therefore have a deep sense of real worth in the sight of God and man, and we have dealt effectively with the problem of hate in our hearts. There is no question that when these enemies in our lives have been cast out by Christ then we can pray effectively. Until they are, then the lines to heaven will continue to be broken and we will wonder why God does not answer prayer. The problem is not with God. Rather, it is with us.

Broken Relationships With Family Or Friends Hamper

Often a person will come to me and say, "Rex, the heavens seem like brass and I cannot pray." Many times I discover the reason is that the person is having trouble at home with his mate, or is having trouble at work with some other person. The Bible says, "Likewise, ye husbands, dwell with them according to knowledge, giving honour unto the wife, as unto the weaker vessel, and as being heirs together of the grace of life; that your prayers be not hindered" (I Peter 3:7).

Broken relationships can have a devastating effect on our prayer lives. When husbands and wives hold grudges they sever their communication with the Creator. When we harbor resentment or ill feelings in our hearts toward another person, then we have broken the line to Heaven. Very truly that person has come between God and ourselves.

Our communication with God has always been linked with our fellowship with man. Jesus said, "And forgive us our debts, as we forgive our debtors" (Matthew 6:12). In the same measure we mete, it is meted to us again. Therefore, if we are to have forgiveness, fellowship, and communication with God, we must clear the air between ourselves. The heavens will always seem like brass when others stand in our way of direct communication.

All of us have seen the tragedy of misunderstandings between believers. Sometimes these broken relationships grow so deep that a whole church suffers. When we permit this to happen, then we have played into the devil's hand. Satan has succeeded in isolating us from not only one another, but also God. And, when we are isolated then we are easy prey for the enemy. Because Jesus knew how vital our relationship one with another is, He simply said, "Forgive us in the same way we forgive others."

Jesus not only warned us about broken relationships, but also told us how to heal them. He said, "Therefore if thou bring thy gift to the altar, and there rememberest that thy brother hath ought against thee; Leave there thy gift before the altar, and go thy way; first be reconciled to thy brother, and then come and offer thy gift" (Matthew 5:23, 24). Jesus goes on to add some very practical advice in getting along with others, "Agree with thine adversary quickly . . ." (Matthew 5:25). Many of us insist so much on having our own ways that we go through life cutting people on the sharp edges of our selfishness. Tragically, we not only harm them but also sever our communication with Christ.

Negative Prayers Produce Negative Answers

One of the most misunderstood points about prayer is that we are dealing with certain of God's laws. God's laws are like His nature—constant, dependable, without flaw and variation. All of our prayers are answered. But, what are we praying? If we pray positive prayers, then we will receive positive answers. However, if we pray negative prayers, we receive negative answers.

Most people who have problems in prayer would do well to examine carefully how they pray. Most usually these pray-ers center on their own weaknesses, shortcomings, and inadequacies. They hold these in focus in prayer until these things become the central theme of that person's talk with God. This is negative praying and will bring only a feeling of self condemnation.

Real and effective praying is moving beyond these negative thoughts to the glorious power of Christ. In other words, we do not center our attention on what we are or how weak we are. Rather, we hold in our prayers what we can become in Christ. It is ridiculous to blame God or prayer power, if we are praying negative prayers, centering our attention on the bad within us or around us, rather than what can happen through Christ.

One day Jesus taught the importance of positive faith in prayer. Matthew records the incident, "And when Jesus departed thence, two blind men followed him, crying, and saying, Thou son of David, have mercy on us. And when he was come into the house, the blind men came to him: and Jesus saith unto them, Believe ye that I am able to do this? They said unto him, Yea, Lord. Then touched he their eyes, saying, According to your faith be it unto you" (Matthew 9:27-29).

Prominent author Charles L. Allen often says, "It

is possible to preach the truth without preaching the gospel." He goes on to say that the "gospel" is "good news" and that is what we should preach. He illustrates his point by noting, "Now, if I preached, 'Diphtheria is a terrible disease that has killed thousands, and ravaged cities,' that is the truth. But, it is not good news. However, if I said, 'Diphtheria is a terrible disease that has killed thousands and ravaged cities; but, medical science has a cure for diphtheria;' now, that is good news." He goes on to add that our preaching cannot be merely a list of the wrongs in our society, but a pointing to Christ who has changed and will change the lives of those in our society.

What is true in preaching is also true in praying. We must move from the negative to the positive in prayer if we are to ever get results. This is the leap of faith that helps us to see what can be in Christ. May we understand that after we have confessed our sins, God is faithful to forgive. And, satan would lock us up in our own feelings of worthlessness until our prayers are small pleas of pity, rather than the powerful force they could be.

Faith Is Moving Into The Arena of Action

Nothing given to us is really ours until we receive it. So it is with our prayers. Until we take that leap of faith and really accept the answer in faith, prayer is merely words. Jesus said, "And all things, whatsoever ye shall ask in prayer, believing, ye shall receive" (Matthew 21:22). Perhaps this aspect of prayer is hardest of all for some.

After we have prayed according to Christ's will with a pure heart and in faith, then we will receive. The answers usually come in unexpected ways but they always come. The wise pray-er will position himself to be ready when the prayer is answered.

We must learn to listen to these answers when they come. Prayer is more than being spiritual chatter-boxes, it is also receiving what Christ wants us to know. God speaks in many voices.

Chapter VI

LEARNING TO LISTEN

"And this is the confidence that we have in him, that, if we ask any thing according to his will, he heareth us"

(I John 5:14).

Pamela Gray has wisely said, "For one soul that exclaims, 'Speak, Lord, for thy servant heareth,' there are ten that say, 'Hear, Lord! For thy servant speaketh!' "

Communication with God is a two-way street if we are to receive maximum benefit in prayer. We must learn to listen to God if we even hear the answers to our needs. Therefore, it would be wise to consider how God speaks to us in answer to our pleas.

Thousands testify that prayer changes things and people. Yet, many struggle with the problem of how God answers prayers. There is an art to listening to God. The language of God has many voices and His Word suggests various ways He speaks in answer to deeper prayers of our spirit. The psalmist said, "Be still, and know that I am God . . ." (Psalm 46:10). There are times we must tune our spiritual ears to His voice and learn of the Lord.

The Bible says, "The heavens declare the glory of God; and the firmament sheweth his handywork. Day unto day uttereth speech, and night unto night sheweth knowledge. There is no speech nor language, where their voice is not heard" (Psalm 19:1-3).

God speaks through His creation. Several things

are told us through the creation. The first is concerning God's eternal power.

The writer of Romans states, "For the invisible things of him from the creation of the world are clearly seen, being understood by the things that are made, even his eternal power and Godhead; so that they are without excuse" (Romans 1:20). God's careful creation speaks of His concern and care. One who provides for His creation is well able to forgive and forget sins. Certainly the Power to speak worlds into existence can speak words of forgiveness to sinful hearts and guilty souls.

God's faithfulness is also expressed. Creation and nature eloquently speak of the faithfulness of a loving God. Jeremiah said, "It is of the Lord's mercies that we are not consumed, because his compassions fail not. They are new every morning: great is thy faithfulness" (Lamentations 3:22, 23). What if one morning dawn did not come. What if fall refused to follow summer and what if rain would not stop, or snow continued until all the world was smothered. We know this can never be, because God faithfully ordained a life-sustaining balance in nature for our protection.

God's tender love is also told us through nature. Jesus called on creation to share eternal truths. One day, speaking about worry, He noted: "Behold the fowls of the air: for they sow not, neither do they reap, nor gather into barns; yet your heavenly Father feedeth them. Are ye not much better than they?" (Matthew 6:26). Driving His point deeper He spread hands across flowered fields, "And why take ye thought for raiment? Consider the lilies of the field, how they grow; they toil not, neither do they spin: And yet I say unto you, That even Solomon in all his glory was not arrayed like one of these. Wherefore, if God so clothe the grass of the field, which to day is, and to morrow is cast into the oven, shall he not much more clothe you, O ye of little faith?" (Matthew 6:28-30). Jesus further illustrates God's care by saying, "Are not five sparrows sold for two farthings, and not one of them is forgotten before God? But even the very hairs of your head are all numbered. Fear not therefore: ye are of more value than many sparrows" (Luke 12:6, 7).

Proverbs notes, "Faithful are the wounds of a friend; but the kisses of an enemy are deceitful" (Proverbs 27:6). Advice and information from our friends is often how God answers us. David's encounter with Nathan is an example.

By way of a parable of two men, one rich with many sheep, one poor with a single, loved sheep, Nathan aroused anger in David's heart. The shepherd king asks, "What kind of man would take the only lamb of a poor man?" Then, demanding justice, David declares, "As the Lord liveth, the man that hath done this thing shall surely die". Friend Nathan replies, "Thou art the man!" Conviction seizes David's heart concerning his sin with Bathsheba (II Samuel 12:1-4). Hot tears roll down his face and David cannot eat or sleep until he receives forgiveness. Psalm 51 is his deep cry for God's love to be restored. Nathan loved David enough that he was faithful in delivering God's message to him.

There is another situation recorded in New Testament Scriptures. One of the shabby times in Peter's life was when he lived by a double standard. Church fathers were arguing how many Jewish rites to retain in Christian worship. Circumcision seemed to be the key issue and Peter vacillated between two extremes of the issue. Paul, a dear friend, records, "But when Peter was come to Antioch, I withstood him to the face, because he was to be blamed . . . I said unto Peter before them all, If thou, being a

Jew, livest after the manner of Gentiles, and not as do the Jews, why compellest thou the Gentiles to live as do the Jews?" (Galatians 2:11, 14).

Friend Paul spoke to Philemon for the runaway slave, Onesimus. He asked that he adopt a proper attitude of forgiveness. Friend Paul loved members of the infant church so much that he often wounded them in order that they might see their errors. At other times he praised them highly. Always he felt God using him to speak to His friends about God's highest will. Paul's single desire was, "That he would grant you, according to the riches of his glory, to be strengthened with might by his Spirit in the inner man" (Ephesians 3:16).

Of course there is a danger in listening to our friends without evaluating their advice. Often they can be honestly mistaken about God's will. The story of God's nameless prophet from Judah in I Kings 13, warns of the tragedy of taking bad advice. The words of an elderly prophet were heeded rather than the explicit instructions of God. Tragedy resulted. God sometimes speaks through friends, but their advice must be weighed carefully in the light of God's Word.

No one is really sure who the first preacher was. Perhaps Noah could rightly be called the first preacher in the modern-day sense. God has chosen to speak to man through anointed messengers of His Word. Paul asks, "How then shall they call on him in whom they have not believed? and how shall they believe in him of whom they have not heard? and how shall they hear without a preacher? And how shall they preach, except they be sent? as it is written, How beautiful are the feet of them that preach the gospel of peace, and bring glad tidings of good things" (Romans 10:14, 15).

Privilege demands responsibility for Jesus said, ". . . unto whomsoever much is given, of him shall much be required . . ." (Luke 12:48). At least three Bible chapters, Jeremiah 23, Zechariah 11, and Ezekiel 34, deal specifically with the responsibility of the clergy.

God speaks through his preachers and their words must be heeded. We preachers, in turn, must recognize that our position demands more than average commitment. God in His love has chosen preachers to communicate that love to His people—". . . it pleased God by the foolishness of preaching to save them that believe" (I Corinthians 1:21). Paul, recognizing this responsibility, states emphatically, "And my speech and my preaching was not with enticing words of man's wisdom, but in demonstration of the Spirit and of power: That your faith should not stand in the wisdom of men, but in the power of God" (I Corinthians 2:4, 5).

One day Philip asked Christ to tell him what God is like. To this Christ replied, ". . . Have I been so long time with you, and yet hast thou not known me, Philip? he that hath seen me hath seen the Father . . ." (John 14:9). Christ is the reflection of the Father.

Hebrews says, "God, who at sundry times and in divers manners spake in time past unto the fathers by the prophets, Hath in these last days spoken unto us by his Son . . ." (Hebrews 1:1, 2).

Many of our prayers have already been answered in the example of the life Christ led. Qualities we must develop have been shown in the life of our Lord. Indeed, God has spoken and is speaking through His Son. We can easily learn methods of evangelism, decisions for our prayer life, how to act and react in crises, and all other lessons of life from the account the Lord left in the Gospels.

The Bible is important for answered prayer. Jesus gave high esteem to the written Word. John adds by saying, "In the beginning was the Word, and the Word was with God, and the Word was God" (John 1:1).

Appropriately, the longest chapter in the Bible is a hymn in praise of God's Word, Psalm 119. The Word was the foundation philosophy of all the prophets and New Testament preachers. Paul admonished Timothy to be adept in the Word while the psalmist David outlines the value of the Word. David states there are six vital values of the Word.

The Word, David notes, is for teaching, "The law of the Lord is perfect, converting the soul." It is also viewed as testimony, "Making wise the simple." The examples of those who followed and those who failed to follow are ample testimony of the Word's value. David understood the Word also as a prescription, filling one with joy and justice; as commandments to avoid moral defilements; as an object of reverence; and as ordinances of righteousness. Paul adds that the Word is profitable for doctrine, reproof, correction, and instruction in righteousness.

Some men, such as Samuel, Moses, and Abraham, have had the privilege of hearing God's audible voice. Others (Jacob, Daniel, and Joseph) have had angelic visitors. Some (Peter, James, and John) walked with Christ in the flesh. But we in our day have the privilege of an even greater understanding of His voice and direction through His words. Christ told skeptical Thomas, ". . . because thou hast seen me, thou hast believed: blessed are they that have not seen, and yet have believed" (John 20:29).

God is speaking in various tongues to His people today. May we have an ear to hear what the Spirit is saying to the church. An old Indian proverb says, "Be silent lest thy tongue keep thee deaf." In these times we need to tune our ear to His voice and then make decisions.

It is true that most prayers have already been answered and all we need do is seek to hear God's voice and direction. From the most general problem to the most specific, God has faithfully heard and answered His people. Prayer works as we are receptive to His answers.

Chapter VII

HOW JESUS PRAYED

"Let us draw near with a true heart in full assurance of faith, having our hearts sprinkled from an evil conscience, and our bodies washed with pure water"

(Hebrews 10:22).

Very little was written about Jesus by His contemporaries. We have only four short Gospels, none of which include a physical description of Jesus, His family status, or His financial position. Secular history of that time adds very little information. There was a purported letter from Pilate to Rome about Jesus, giving a physical description, but scholars are very skeptical about its validity.

Josephus, the Jewish historian of that era, had very little to say about Christ. In his huge work of history, he only mentions, "There was about this time Jesus, a wise man, if it be lawful to call him a man, for he was a doer of wonderful works. He was Christ. Pilate, at the suggestion of the principal man among us, condemned him to the cross. He appeared to his followers alive again the third day." Beyond this, secular history adds little about Jesus.

Surprisingly, the Gospels give very few details about the prayer life of our Lord. It is mentioned frequently that He prayed, sometimes all night long. But, not much space is given to record the prayers He prayed. However, one whole chapter of John's Gospel does preserve one of His eloquent prayers and we can learn much from it for our own prayer lives. In that powerful prayer Christ makes certain requests for those who would follow Him. And, He did not have just the disciples in mind when He prayed. The Bible says, "Neither pray I for these alone, but for them also which shall believe on me through their word" (John 17:20). Thus, we are included in Christ's prayer.

When Jesus prayed during those short days before His death, there were five specific things He requested for His followers. Because these were His deepest desires for us in His prayer, they should also form the crux of our prayers. Jesus prayed we might have unity, joy, protection, purity, and eternal life.

That They Might Be One

At the very beginning of Christ's prayer He mentioned the exclusiveness of it; "I pray for them: I pray not for the world, but for them which thou hast given me; for they are thine" (John 17:9). Therefore, we are made aware this prayer is a very personal plea for the ones Jesus loves. After Christ praises the Father He then moves to acknowledge how He has fulfilled God's will and then goes on to pray for us.

Appropriately, the first request Jesus makes is, ". . . Holy Father, keep through thine own name those whom thou hast given me, that they may be one, as we are" (John 17:11). Before the end of His prayer Jesus would repeat this request twice because of its importance. Satan has splintered the church and divided brother against brother. This was never the will of our Lord. His careful prayer was that we always be one in spirit and unity. In isolating us from one another, satan has destroyed much of our effectiveness.

From the very beginning of His ministry, Jesus let us know the urgency of unity. He clearly said,

"A new commandment I give unto you, That ye love one another; as I have loved you, that ye also love one another. By this shall all men know that ye are my disciples, if ye have love one to another" (John 13:34, 35). A divided church in a divided world speaks nothing but disharmony. Therefore, the first prayer all of us must pray is that we be made one in love and spirit. While we may worship in different congregations with different denominational labels we still must have that deep feeling of oneness and love for each other. We are brothers, not competitors. We too long have been asking people to change churches, rather than sinners to change direction.

The only legitimate testimony we have is that we love one another. The world is choking on religion with each new sect seeking for the attention of men. The one faith set apart from all others is the one which reconciles man to God and man to man. Therefore, Jesus prayed that we might be one, even as He and the Father are one. We must pray to love one another more and then put legs on our prayers by doing just that.

Joy With Our Salvation

Strangely, the second request of our Lord is that we have joy. "And now come I to thee; and these things I speak in the world, that they might have my joy fulfilled in themselves" (John 17:13). Somewhere along the line a lot of us have gotten the wrong impression about salvation. A lot of people think it is a sad life with little joy. How wrong they are. Jesus wants us to have life and life more abundantly.

Jesus knew exactly what He was saying when He placed this request second in the list of desires for His people. He knew joy is necessary if we ever live a successful Christian life and be a witness for Him. Nehemiah, while rebuilding the walls of Jerusalem, said, ". . . for the joy of the Lord is your strength" (Nehemiah 8:10). As long as Nehemiah was pouting in the palace, he got nothing done for God. But, when God filled Him with vision and he began to work in joy, the job was finished. There are many anemic and weak Christians who continually are defeated because they lack joy in their lives. They mope through their spiritual lives while others thrive in the presence of the King. The difference is that the strong have joy while the weak do not.

Joy is necessary not only to give strength to face battles and trials, but also for effective witness. David recognized that one who has lost his joy cannot share God with anyone. He said, "Restore unto me the joy of thy salvation; and uphold me with thy free spirit. Then will I teach transgressors thy ways; and sinners shall be converted unto thee" (Psalm 51:12, 13). Isaiah adds to this by saying, "Therefore with joy shall ye draw water out of the wells of salvation" (Isaiah 12:3). Many people have a hard time leading souls to Christ because their joy is gone. No wonder Jesus prayed that we might have His joy fulfilled in us. And this should be high on our prayer priority list.

Paul tells us the fruit of the Spirit is joy. Growing out of a life in Christ can come that joy. The seed was planted at salvation. Through prayer we cause the joy to grow and we become strong Christians and powerful soul winners. The Bible says, "Thou wilt shew me the path of life: in thy presence is fulness of joy; at thy right hand there are pleasures for evermore" (Psalm 16:11). Joy does more than make us feel good, it gives strength and helps us witness.

Petition For Protection

Carl Sandburg has said, "When I doubt there is an evil one, I have only to look into myself and there he is." Always sitting on the doorstep of our lives lurks the devil. He desires to destroy us and for this reason Jesus requested, "I pray not that thou shouldest take them out of the world, but that thou shouldest keep them from the evil" (John 17:15).

One day Jesus looked deep into the eyes of Simon Peter and said, ". . . Satan hath desired to have you, that he may sift you as wheat" (Luke 22:31). No doubt chills ran up and down Peter's spine when he heard these words. He had seen the tragedy of those caught in the clutches of the devil. He had seen those driven by demons and tormented by sickness. He had associated with those who were caught in the claws of sin. Panic probably choked Peter until he also heard Christ say, "But I have prayed for thee, that thy faith fail not: and when thou art converted, strengthen thy brethren" (Luke 22:32). It makes all the difference in the world when Christ prays for us.

We are no match for satan. He is subtle and deceitful and often we can be tempted to fall for his wiles. For this reason our Lord has prayed that our faith fail not. The wise person will take this cue and pray daily for protection from the evil one. It is true that most of us do not flee temptation. Rather, we crawl away, hoping it will overcome us. Because we are so weak and short-sighted in these areas, we need the prayerful protection of our Christ.

Paul frankly admitted the plight of man against satan, "For the good that I would I do not: but the evil which I would not, that I do" (Romans 7:19). Paul does not resign himself to helplessness though.

51

Rather, he had found his answer and that was in Christ. He no longer had to serve the law of flesh, but through Christ would rise above the temptations that before defeated him. From a heart of thankfulness, he went on to say, "There is therefore now no condemnation to them which are in Christ Jesus, who walk not after the flesh, but after the Spirit" (Romans 8:1). Christ indeed set us, slaves, free.

That We Be Made Pure

An old preacher made the observation, "Well, maybe I ain't what I ought to be. But, thank God I ain't what I used to be and I ain't what I'm gonna be." That statement captures the desire for our growth Jesus prayed for, when He said, "Sanctify them through thy truth: thy word is truth" (John 17:17).

One day Gideon was threshing wheat in an old wine press. He did the work there because the Midianites ruled the country and were constantly tormenting Israel. They killed them, stole their food, and made slaves of their sons. Suddenly an angel appeared to Gideon and said, ". . . The Lord is with thee, thou mighty man of valour" (Judges 6:12). What a ridiculous scene this seemed to be. Somewhat sarcastically, Gideon answered, ". . . Oh my Lord, if the Lord be with us, why then is all this befallen us? and where be all his miracles which our fathers told us of . . ." (Judges 6:13). Gideon was a victim of his circumstances and did not see at all what the angel was talking about.

God looked at Gideon's situation far differently than Gideon. The Master saw in Gideon what he could become as he yielded his life to the Lord. Gideon only saw himself as a slave in bondage to a pagan people. Only after God continued to deal with Gideon did he begin to realize that Israel could be free again and the miracles of the fathers could be repeated.

In our own lives we are often kept captives by what we see in ourselves. However, God would like for us to look to Him and see what we can become as we yield to His spirit. This is why Jesus prayed we would keep on growing until we are sanctified by truth. Peter had this same experience. Jesus called him to service by saying, ". . . Thou art Simon the son of Jona: thou shalt be called Cephas, which is by interpretation, A stone" (John 1:42). It was not important who Simon was, only who he could become in Christ. It is the same with our lives.

When we learn to pray as Jesus prayed, we will seek to grow to our full potential in Christ. We cannot possibly know at this point what we can become in our Lord. Every day we should pray for this growth.

That We Might Have Eternal Life

When we love someone deeply, we long to be with them. Whenever I have to leave my family I look forward to the time I can again be with them. My life is only really complete when we are together. This was the same spirit Jesus mentioned when He prayed, "Father, I will that they also, whom thou hast given me, be with me where I am; that they may behold my glory, which thou hast given me: for thou lovedst me before the foundation of the world" (John 17:24).

What a grand way to end the prayer of Christ. In that last plea we begin to see just how much we mean to Him. What Christ is actually saying is that Heaven will not be complete until we are with Him forever. It is almost more than we can imagine that our great God loves us so much He wishes us to be with Him forever. No wonder Isaiah heard God say, "Can a woman forget her sucking child, that she should not have compassion on the son of her womb? yea, they may forget, yet will I not forget thee" (Isaiah 49:15).

With such a deep knowledge of Christ's love for us, we have a healthy confidence to live and a longing to share our Lord with our fellow man. And, when we learn how Christ prayed, we can imitate His prayer and more perfectly fulfill the will of our Father. As Jesus, we must pray for unity among ourselves, joy to be part of our lives, protection from the evil one, purity of heart, and that Jesus come quickly so we might share in His eternity with Him.

Understanding the love of our Lord, we must also recognize our responsibility to tell others about our Christ. God's Word says, "And the Spirit and the bride say, Come . . ." (Revelation 22:17). God's Spirit invites the sinner. Christ's Bride is to give the invitation. The Bible tells us we who are saved are the Bride of Christ. Therefore, the commission is clear. We have an urgent responsibility to invite the world to Jesus.

Chapter VIII

PATTERN OF PRAYER

"After this manner therefore pray ye: Our Father which art in heaven, Hallowed be thy name. Thy kingdom come. Thy will be done in earth, as it is in heaven. Give us this day our daily bread. And forgive us our debts, as we forgive our debtors. And lead us not into temptation, but deliver us from evil: For thine is the kingdom, and the power, and the glory, for ever. Amen"

(Matthew 6:9-13).

Several years ago a highly-sophisticated study of prayer was made by the psychology department of Redlands University. Under the direction of Dr. William R. Parker, exciting observations were made concerning prayer power. Explaining the study later, Dr. Parker said, "Our work differed not only in our academic approach but in our emphasis. Church groups have been attempting to incorporate psychology and prayer. But so much emphasis has been put on the 'ology' that conclusions in many instances led to a mistaken idea that power lay in these types of therapy. Our experiments proved the power lay with God."

The prominent doctor went on to add, "No one in our class was healed or helped by the power of the group, the application of psychology, nor by myself as a leader . . . But the healing power lay in a God of love which each student found by 'going into the closet and shutting the door.'"

More people each day are beginning to learn the

power of prayer. Medical Doctor Howard A. Rusk noted, "One could not practice 'rehabilitation' if he did not believe in God and prayer." He went on to say, "How and when the ability to pray comes, how the prayer is offered and how the individual attains oneness with God, differs in each one." While we would agree with the doctor about each individual finding God in a different way, still there is a pattern to powerful praying. Christ taught it, and this is known as the "Lord's Prayer." It is a simple formula for bringing prayer power to our lives.

Recorded twice in Scripture, what is known as the "Lord's Prayer" is actually His believer's prayer. It is the prayer He taught us to pray and through it gain a deeper knowledge of God and His will. Divided into ten short sections, the prayer can be easily memorized by all. However, this is not the purpose. Rather, it forms an outline of prayer and we are to add our own words from our deep feelings. It is carefully structured by our Lord to show us exactly how to pray.

Our Father . . .

Jesus established a relationship of love between the believer and his God. Just as an earthly father is easy to entreat, so the heavenly Father listens and loves. We are not heard for our much speaking; rather, because He loves and wants to give. Christ added in His famous discourse on prayer, "Or what man is there of you, whom if his son ask bread, will he give him a stone? Or if he ask a fish, will he give him a serpent? If ye then, being evil, know how to give good gifts unto your children, how much more shall your Father which is in heaven give good things to them that ask him?" (Matthew 7:9-11). Therefore, the believer approaches the great God in a loving family relationship.

. . . Which Art In Heaven,
Hallowed Be Thy Name . . .

While God is our Father, He still is God and deserves our respect. By recognizing His position we recognize His ability to assist us far beyond the help of any earthly father. Our familiarity with God in a family relationship should not lessen our respect and reverence. Rather, it will deepen it. Therefore, Christ taught us early in each prayer to pause and thank God for that relationship recognizing His great glory. Praise is in its proper place when it both begins and ends our petitions.

. . . Thy Kingdom Come . . .

This world has been wrecked by the havoc of satan. Christ teaches us to pray that His kingdom will come in the hearts of men and on the face of this earth. This happens in two ways. First, as men turn to Christ and discover His Kingdom within, their world changes. They no longer live to "get" but live to "give." They become kind and loving individuals who change their world through expressions of sacrifice and service. Then, too, this prayer looks forward to the day when Christ shall come in all His glory. Then, there will be no more wars, famines, heartbreaks or pain. Every Christian everywhere should pray daily for Christ's Kingdom to come. All of creation groans for that release.

. . . Thy Will Be Done In Earth,
As It Is In Heaven . . .

For some eternal reason God has tied His hands on earth. He has involved us in the redemptive process so that whatever we bind on earth shall be bound in heaven and whatever we loose on earth shall be loosed in heaven. This mysterious truth simply means that God works as we pray. We have all seen the tragedy of war and heartbreak when God's will is not done on earth. Therefore, each prayer should be one imploring God to bring forces to bear on this earth so men will be responsive to His glorious will. This also means that our own hearts are made aware that often our will contradicts His. As we pray His will be done, we bend our will to that Eternal One.

. . . Give Us This Day, Our Daily Bread . . .

God desires we ask Him each day for our daily needs. Martin Luther observed, "Even though God may well provide these blessings without our asking, He wants us to acknowledge that they come from him." So often we reluctantly ask God for material blessings. Yet, in the prayer Christ taught us to pray, it is very clear the Father desires this type of petition. Many Old Testament saints understood this premise. The Psalmist prayed, ". . . O Lord, I beseech thee, send now prosperity" (Psalm 118: 25). Nehemiah frankly asked, "O Lord, I beseech thee, let now thine ear be attentive to the prayer of thy servant, and to the prayer of thy servants, who desire to fear thy name: and prosper, I pray thee, thy servant this day . . ." (Nehemiah 1:11).

God has impressed me lately with the fact He wants this ministry to have money. We are thoroughly dedicated to Him and our only desire is to win souls. Therefore, I feel free to pray this prayer of prosperity. And, all Christians everywhere, as long as they will use the money for the Kingdom, should pray this same prayer of prosperity. Then, the work of the Kingdom can be accomplished. Dare to believe God for your daily bread. Your life level will change when you take this commanded step of faith.

. . . And Forgive Us Our Debts,
As We Forgive Our Debtors . . .

We have already seen how our forgiveness is predicated on our ability to forgive. This part of the prayer Christ taught simply calls attention to our moral duty toward the family of man. We cannot go through life hurting and harming others and expect to keep clear communication with the Father. Jesus reduced all commandments to two: Love God with all your heart, and your neighbor as yourself. Our relationship with God is in the form of a triangle. It not only includes God and ourselves, but also reaches to our fellowman.

. . . And Lead Us Not Into Temptation . . .

While the spirit is willing, the flesh is weak. Christ teaches us to pray that we escape temptation; while we might stand the test of trial, Jesus taught here that we should desire deliverance from the test if possible. It is the same principle as a drunkard being saved from alcohol, but still going to the tavern each day to prove his strength. One day he probably will not be able to continue resisting, and will fall back to drink. Jesus is simply saying it is better to see how far away from sin we can live, rather than flirting with our lower nature. We need to pray God will help us be wise enough to shun temptation.

. . . But Deliver Us From Evil . . .

Almost in the same breath this prayer follows the preceeding thought. Here we are praying for complete deliverance from that evil one who has choked our world to its knees and bred hatred and war among mankind. God's Word tells us there will come a day when this world will be redeemed to God and when that happens all the havoc of satan will be destroyed. It is to be replaced by the glorious Kingdom of Christ. This is another plea for that Kingdom to come to set man and creation free. Our daily cry is that the agony of this earth be shortened and our Lord return.

. . . For Thine Is The Kingdom, And The Power, And The Glory, For Ever . . .

Jesus now comes to the full circle of prayer. Note, this prayer began with praise, and now concludes with it. While the evil one does have power, still we recognize ". . . greater is he that is in you, than he that is in the world" (I John 4:4). It is our Father who is all-powerful and full of glory. Here we express the confidence that ultimately evil will be conquered and Christ will reign for ever and ever. This is the hope awaiting the believer. It is a hope based on the truth of God's power, glory, and goodness. Our prayers must be full of praise and hope if they rise to full power.

. . . Amen

This final note in the Lord's prayer is one of confidence that the Lord has heard us. We do not speak empty words into empty air. Rather, we have the Divine assurance that what we ask in Christ's name will be done. Thus, a resounding "Amen" fills the end of our prayer.

This pattern of effective praying can change your life. Note again, it recognizes a loving relationship, reveres our Father, moves to concern for the lost world, asks for God's will to be done in earth and our lives, prays for prosperity, asks forgiveness for sins, deliverance from temptation and evil, finishes in praise and assurance. No wonder this prayer has meant so much to so many and has indeed taught millions how to pray. It covers all needs of the soul and body and lifts our hearts to the heart of God.

Chapter IX

PRAISE WITH A PROMISE

"But ye are a chosen generation, a royal priesthood, an holy nation, a peculiar people; that ye should shew forth the praises of him who hath called you out of darkness into his marvellous light:"

(I Peter 2:9).

Many nights, flying home from television rallies we conduct all over North America, I watch the lights of the huge cities slide slowly beneath the plane. In those quiet moments I often pause to praise God for the witness we have there through our television ministry. Long ago I learned that praise is a vital part of prayer. Therefore, in addition to praying for the souls in these cities, I also praise God because He has helped us reach so many.

A lot of people are limited in their prayer lives because they have not yet learned the power of praise. They too often view prayer as a time to turn in a list of their needs, much like a small child would write a letter to Santa Claus. Prayer is much more than requesting things; it is communication with the Creator in thanksgiving, supplication, and cooperation. The effective pray-er will make praise a vital part of each prayer.

God's Word tells us there are at least four important reasons we praise God in prayer. They are: Praise touches God's glory, Praise focuses on the possibility rather than the problem, Praise cooperates with God's purpose, and Praise has a promise.

Praise Touches God's Glory

For a long time Israel had wanted to build a temple for their God. David yearned to build it, but God said it would be David's son, Solomon, who would have that unique privilege. Years of careful work finally brought about the most beautiful building man had ever erected. The day of dedication came and Israel rejoiced in the magnificence of the structure.

Great choirs and orchestras had been prepared for this exciting occasion. The Levites had practiced long. The priests tensed with excitement as the ceremonies began. Solomon was to lead in prayer on this day of days. The worship service started and the pomp and glory was all they had anticipated.

The Ark was brought in and the priests entered the holy place. When they came out the singers started their beautiful hymn of praise. The Bible says, "It came even to pass, as the trumpeters and singers were as one, to make one sound to be heard in praising and thanking the Lord; and when they lifted up their voice with the trumpets and cymbals and instruments of musick, and praised the Lord, saying, For he is good; for his mercy endureth for ever: that then the house was filled with a cloud, even the house of the Lord; So that the priests could not stand to minister by reason of the cloud: for the glory of the Lord had filled the house of God" (II Chronicles 5:13, 14).

It should be noted that God's glory was touched when the people began praising and thanking the Lord. Thus, Praise touches God's Glory. Imagine the problem the priest had that glorious day. The house was so filled with God's glory the priests could not even minister. I long for a great revival to sweep our land in such a fashion. And, I deeply believe it can come as God's people learn to praise in prayer. The Psalmist added, "But thou art holy, O thou that inhabitest the praises of Israel" (Psalm 22:3).

God lives in the praises of His people. No wonder satan would want us to be selfish in our prayer times and merely submit a list of requests rather than really praise God. This is why we have a great music program in our church, with singers and orchestra members on our staff. We give glory to God with the instruments of music and God, in turn, blesses us with His glory and we see souls saved. I am more deeply aware of the blessings of God on our ministry today than ever before. I believe our praise has touched God's glory.

What can you give a God who has everything? This is the question posed by the Psalmist when he asked, "What shall I render unto the Lord for all his benefits toward me?" (Psalm 116:12). In response to his own question, he answers, "I will offer to thee the sacrifice of thanksgiving, and will call upon the name of the Lord" (Psalm 116:17). It is thrilling to know that we can give God something He does not have; the praise of our hearts. And, when we offer this expression of love to our Lord, we touch His glory.

In our age of guided missiles and misguided men, we need more than ever the touch, the glory, of the Lord. Perhaps it would be well to stop our pleadings for a moment and start a great chorus of praise to reach that glory. The Psalmist also reminded, "Whoso offereth praise glorifieth me: and to him that ordereth his conversation aright will I shew the salvation of God" (Psalm 50:23). Could it be that the revival we seek for the souls of men is wrapped up in the power of praise? I think so and encourage you to touch God's glory with your thankful heart.

Praise Focuses On The Possibility
Rather Than The Problem

When Gideon was threshing wheat down in that winepress, the angel came calling him a mighty man of valour. Gideon was so wrapped up in Israel's problems he could not even see the possibility of victory. I felt much the same way when my ministry was recently attacked publicly. However, after those eight days of fasting and prayer God helped me to focus my faith on the possibility rather than the problem. And, from that, there has been a new touch from God on my life.

We get so embroiled with the nitty-gritty of everyday life it is hard for us to look beyond our needs to see His provision. Praise is a potent tool to help us move from the negative to the positive. As long as we are locked in the prison of our limitations then we cannot perform the ministry God has called us to. Therefore, praise with prayer is vital if we are to accomplish anything for our Lord.

Paul understood this principle of faith. He wrote to the Philippians, "Be careful for nothing; but in every thing by prayer and supplication with thanksgiving let your requests be made known unto God. And the peace of God, which passeth all understanding, shall keep your hearts and minds through Christ Jesus" (Philippians 4:6, 7). The great apostle simply told the people not to fret about the cares of life, but, through prayer with praise, move to the arena of faith. When this is done, the great peace settles into our souls.

I have seen this principle of faith work many times in my ministry. Often, standing at the deathbed of a great Christian, or in the hospital, I have seen these people turn their faith loose through prayer with praise and God bring a healing to their spirits that the doctors could not even understand.

Hooked to this matter of praying with praise, Paul goes on to add, "Finally, brethren, whatsoever things are true, whatsoever things are honest, whatsoever things are just, whatsoever things are pure, whatsoever things are lovely, whatsoever things are of good report; if there be any virtue, and if there be any praise, think on these things" (Philippians 4:8).

Sometimes when you ask a person how he is doing, he will reply, "Well, I guess I'm doing okay, under the circumstances." Usually that is exactly where he is, "under the circumstances." Praise helps us rise above the circumstances looking beyond the problem to the possibility. Therefore the dynamic Christian and effective soulwinner will praise God in prayer and move to a more meaningful ministry.

Praise Helps Us Understand God's Will

God could have saved Israel from the famine through another way than Joseph having to suffer slavery and imprisonment. I am convinced that all that happening to Joseph was not as God would have planned it. No doubt Joseph's brothers will be held eternally responsible for their part in selling their brother into slavery. However, the point is that even though these terrible circumstances surrounded Joseph, God took them and turned them into a great and noble purpose.

Often we get ourselves entangled with many things that are not of God's first will. Then, when these things almost drown us, we turn to God and find He can indeed bring order out of chaos. This was exactly what Paul meant when he wrote, "And we know that all things work together for good to them that love God, to them who are the called according to his purpose" (Romans 8:28).

In other words, God can and will bring the best out of our worst if we but trust Him.

Praise helps us recognize God's ability to change things. If we really understand this, then we will not get panic-stricken when the world seems to crash about us. The wise pray-er will, in those moments, say, "Lord, I did not wish this to happen, but I am convinced that You will bring the best from it." With such faith, we grow into the persons God desires us to be.

It is important for us to understand that our praise is not predicated on conditions, but on God's goodness. If we praise God only when things are going well, then our praise life will be erratic as the waves of the sea. However, God's Word says we are to praise God at all times for:

The greatness of God: "Praise him for his mighty acts: praise him according to his excellent greatness" (Psalm 150:2).

The goodness of God: "Praise ye the Lord. O give thanks unto the Lord; for he is good: for his mercy endureth for ever" (Psalm 106:1).

The salvation of God: "Behold, God is my salvation; I will trust, and not be afraid: for the Lord Jehovah is my strength and my song; he also is become my salvation" (Isaiah 12:2).

Victory through Christ: "But thanks be to God, which giveth us the victory through our Lord Jesus Christ" (I Corinthians 15:57).

When a person recognizes his praise is predicated on God's goodness, rather than circumstances, then praise and prayer can roll from our lips even though all seems black around us. This is the type of faith that is deeper than death, stronger than trial, and made Paul cry out, "For I am persuaded, that neither death, nor life, nor angels, nor principalities, nor powers, nor things present, nor things to come, Nor height, nor depth, nor any other creature, shall be able to separate us from the love of God, which is in Christ Jesus our Lord" (Romans 8:38, 39).

Praise Has A Promise

There is another vital reason we praise God in prayer. And that is, there is a precious and powerful promise associated with praise. God's Word declares, "Delight thyself also in the Lord; and he shall give thee the desires of thine heart" (Psalm 37:4). Isaiah repeated this promise by saying, "Then shalt thou delight thyself in the Lord; and I will cause thee to ride upon the high places of the earth, and feed thee with the heritage of Jacob thy father: for the mouth of the Lord hath spoken it" (Isaiah 58:14).

It is true that as we delight ourselves in the Lord, our will melts into His. We become more and more like Christ and the desires of our hearts become intertwined into a deep compassion for the lost of this world. What a promise this is. If we learn to praise God and delight ourselves in Him then the longing of our souls will be met. Again, we must recognize that the revival of souls we have prayed for might just be wrapped up in the power of praise.

Chapter X

WHERE YOU ARE
WITH WHAT YOU HAVE

*"Withhold not good from them to whom it is due,
when it is in the power of thine hand to do it"*
(Proverbs 3:27).

One day a fellow from West Virginia came up to
see the Cathedral of Tomorrow. He was a circuit-
riding preacher, one of the last of that special breed
of men who travel to various preaching points sharing the gospel. He had a jeep and served as pastor
of five little Methodist churches. They collectively
did not pay him enough to support his family, so
he worked in the coal mines during the week, and
used the weekends to perform his ministry.

I happened to see him standing under the big
cross of the Cathedral after everyone else had left
the service. He started to cry. I overheard him say,
"I wish I could build something like this for God so
that when I stand in His presence, I can be proud
of what I've done." My heart was deeply moved
and I said, "But, you've got this whole thing wrong.
Maybe God let me have this big Cathedral and
these open doors of television and I haven't been as
faithful as I could with the tools I've had in my
hands."

Explaining further, I felt impressed to share with
him, "You just told me you had to dig coal and sell
it to keep body and soul together, and buy gas to go
to your five churches. I wonder if I would go to
West Virginia and were in your place, if I would
stay in faith . . . No, brother, I wouldn't be a bit
surprised when we get home to heaven, you're going to find out the Lord has a bigger reward for you
than He has for me."

This old-fashioned Methodist preacher just took off up and down the aisles crying, praising God, and clapping his hands. My dad used to call it a "running fit." There was no one in the Cathedral but this fellow and myself. When he got through rejoicing he said, "I'm going back to West Virginia and I'm going to be more faithful than I've ever been because that's where God has placed me."

When each of us learns that God has placed us in certain positions for His greatest glory and good, then we can do more where we are with what we have. A lot of people build air castles by dreaming of what they could do if they were in another place or had another ministry. I deeply believe God knows exactly what He is doing when He gives each of us our own ministries. God never said we were to be successful in men's eyes. Rather, He said, "Moreover it is required in stewards, that a man be found faithful" (I Corinthians 4:2). What an exciting premise this is! We are rewarded for what we do with what we have.

Ministry Of Helps

God has placed many prominent ministries in the church. There are the gifts of miracles, healings, knowledge, and wisdom. Explaining this Paul says, "And God hath set some in the church, first apostles, secondarily prophets, thirdly teachers, after that miracles, then gifts of healings, helps, governments, diversities of tongues" (I Corinthians 12:28). While we recognize the more glamorous ministries, we often overlook the urgency of the ministry of helps.

I often think of that night when Paul the apostle had to slip from the city to save his life. Somebody had to hold that basket as he was let down over the wall. That person's name is never mentioned, but what a tremendous ministry he had in holding the rope.

All of us remember names like Paul, Peter, James, John. However, there are lesser names we forget because we glamorize the dramatic gifts. Hidden in Scripture is the name, Onesiphorus. Probably very few readers will recognize this name. Yet, his ministry of helps lifted Paul in his hour of deepest need, and encouraged the apostle when he was tempted to give up. Paul wrote fondly to young Timothy, "The Lord give mercy unto the house of Onesiphorus; for he oft refreshed me, and was not ashamed of my chain: But, when he was in Rome, he sought me out very diligently, and found me. The Lord grant unto him that he may find mercy of the Lord in that day: and in how many things he ministered unto me at Ephesus, thou knowest very well" (II Timothy 1:16-18).

Because we recognize the urgency of those laborers with us, we ask for faithful stewards. This means doing all we can, where we are, for the glory of God. This was the same attitude David recognized in I Samuel 30:24, "For who will hearken unto you in this matter? but as his part is that goeth down to the battle, so shall his part be that tarrieth by the stuff: they shall part alike." Those who fight the battle of faith on the front lines receive their rewards. And, those who provide for the fighters and "stay by the stuff," share alike in the victory.

Paul recognized those who made his dramatic ministry possible. He once said, "Now he that ministereth seed to the sower both minister bread for your food, and multiply your seed sown, and increase the fruits of your righteousness;) Being enriched in every thing to all bountifulness, which causeth through us thanksgiving to God" (II Corinthians 9:10, 11). There is an exciting ministry of providing seed to the sower.

Getting the gospel out costs money. I do not believe it is God's will for the world to have a corner on the money market and thus hamper the work of the Kingdom. Therefore, we are boldly asking God's people everywhere to give what they can, where they are, to bring great blessing to the world through this ministry.

God has caused me to change my thinking concerning finances. I believe now that God has placed many thousands of Christians in a financial place where they can support this ministry to the lost. When God called Noah to preach and build, Noah needed the money to do so. God provided him with it. He was probably a rich man who could afford to hire the workers, and give himself completely to the task of preaching and preparing. So today, God is providing for this ministry through those who are faithful stewards.

Opening Our Hearts

It is incomprehensible that Christ would give us a commandment to go and preach the gospel to every creature, without making provision to provide seed to the sower. If our hearts and purposes are right, God will see to it, through his faithful stewards, that the needs of the ministry be met. I believe God is speaking and will speak to hearts about their support of this ministry. By all of us doing our parts, we are going to have the means to expand this ministry around the world. I strongly feel there will be a real moral awakening.

Moral awakening comes through great power. It will be harder and more expensive to preach the gospel in these last days. But I believe God has set before us an open door that no man can close.

May God help his people everywhere to realize the vital part they have in this last-hour revival. If they can be encouraged to work where they are, give sacrificially to the ministry, and use what they have, there is no limit to what can and will be done.

It would be well to read the prophets carefully and see how preoccupied they were with the neglect of God's people to the heartbeat of God and the heartcry of man. Jesus forever settles our responsibility by saying, ". . . For unto whomsoever much is given, of him shall much be required: and to whom men have committed much, of him they will ask the more" (Luke 12:48).

God has so blessed us and for this we are eternally grateful. My deepest prayer is that God will constantly remind us of our responsibilities and wake us with the cries of mankind. May we always be haunted with this refrain:

I wonder have I cared enough for others,
    Or have I let them die alone?
I might have helped a wan-d'rer to the Saviour;
    The seeds of Precious Life I might have sown.
How many are the lost that I have lifted?
    How many are the chains I've helped to free?
I wonder, have I done my best for Jesus,
    When He has done so much for me?

Chapter XI

SEVEN STEPS TO PRAYER POWER

"Pray without ceasing"

(I Thessalonians 5:17).

One day a tourist saw the famed sculptor Rodin at work in Rome. "Oh, Mr. Rodin," she fluttered, "Is it difficult to sculpt?"

"Not at all, Madam," replied the Master. "You simply buy a block of marble and chip away what you don't want." Simple, yes, but not easy.

In learning to be effective in prayer, it is really simple but not always easy. Satan stands in our way to prayer power and so often we are discouraged by our own inadequacies. However, as we are patient we grow in prayer power until God can use us in effective ways. I want to share seven steps that will help you grow into powerful pray-ers.

1. FOLLOW THE FORMULA.

In an earlier chapter we dealt with the formula for prayer that Christ gave. This should be carefully followed as we structure our petitions. There is the temptation to let our prayers slide back to selfish pleadings or demeaning notes of self-condemnation. This is counter-productive, and a waste of time. Simply stated, Christ's formula for effective praying is:

A. Recognize a loving relationship with the Father.

B. Start the prayer with praise and reverence.

ought: but the Spirit itself maketh intercession for us with groanings which cannot be uttered" (Romans 8:26).

7. GIVE TO GAIN.

The final and perhaps the most forceful step to powerful praying is that of giving. We receive only as we give. We must:

A. Give of our time in prayer.
B. Give of ourselves in service.
C. Give of our means to the ministry of winning the lost.

If this final step is taken new power will come into our lives that not only brings blessing to the ministry, but will also give our lives another dimension of faith.

These seven steps to powerful prayer can change lives and bring revival to this lost world. I am believing you will join us in this last hour in reaching men for Christ through prayer power.

C. Pray that Christ's Kingdom will come in the earth and in your life.
D. Ask for God's Will to be done in all things.
E. Pray for prosperity and provision.
F. Ask forgiveness in the same measure you forgive.
G. Pray to be kept from temptation and evil.
H. Conclude the prayer with praise and confidence.

All needs are covered by this formula for both soul and body. Relationships with others are dealt with through this prayer formula. The wise pray-er will use this skeleton on which to build his every prayer.

2. PRAY WITH THE SAME ATTITUDE JESUS HAD.

After we learn the simple formula for prayer, there is the added dimension of attitude. In an earlier chapter we discussed the prayer Christ prayed for His children which included five specific requests. These form attitudes of prayer in the prayer life of our Lord. They are:

A. A spirit of unity and love among all Christians.
B. A joyful relationship with the Father that gives strength and encourages strong witness.
C. Dependence for protection from the enemy of our souls.
D. Understanding that we grow in grace and prayer power.
E. A longing to be with our Lord for evermore.

Unity, joy, dependence, self-acceptance, and a deep love for the Lord form a triangle of power that includes God, our fellow man, and ourselves. When these attitudes grip all our prayer periods, then we will become more dynamic pray-ers.

3. LEARN TO LISTEN.

Remembering that God speaks in many voices, we learn to listen more carefully to His answers to our prayers. God answers us through:

A. His creation.
B. Our spiritual friends.
C. His ministers of the gospel.
D. His Son, Jesus.
E. The Holy Spirit.
F. Through His Word.

Learning to listen to God's answers to our prayers is not as difficult as some would make it. Remember, Christ told John repeatedly, "He that hath an ear, let him hear what the Spirit saith unto the churches" (Revelation 3:22).

4. REMEMBER WHAT WILL SHORT-CIR-CUIT YOUR PRAYERS.

Prayer works on God's laws just as sure as the law of gravity. When we violate one of these laws of prayer, we short-circuit our prayer system and will not receive answers. The laws of prayer are:

A. Prayer works only for those who are saved (John 9:31).
B. Broken relationships with others block the paths of prayer.
C. Negative prayers will get negative results.
D. Faith is moving into action, many times with ourselves being the answers to our own prayers.

When the prayer system has been checked and these laws understood then prayer becomes an open access to God. If we ignore, or if we try to circumvent, these laws, our prayers are empty words spoken into the air.

5. FAST FOR ADDED POWER.

Many people have never experienced the ad dimension of power fasting brings. It was much a part of the Lord's life, and at one tim fasted 40 days and nights. Coming out of tha perience He had an added dimension to His n try not known before. Fasting:

A. Denies the flesh and helps keep the bod der subjection.
B. Gives added power to the believer (M 17:20, 21).
C. Brings exciting results when regular p seems to fail.

I believe revival will come in our day, b forces are so strong God's people need to the added dimension of power in their n

6. PRACTICE PRAYER DAILY.

Prayer must not be used as a fire escape, like an emergency letter to home asking for It must be a vital part of each day's activ are to become powerful pray-ers. I sugges

A. Pray before each day starts.
B. Pray before retiring at night.
C. Remember that prayer is more th tivity, it is an attitude. Thus, we without ceasing.
D. Remind ourselves of the four dim prayer (Supplications, communic pleadings, giving of thanks).

It would be well to remember the mo the more power we have in prayer. F like gasoline, in danger of running out i far. It is more like a muscle which stren practice. As we pray it is comforting t "Likewise the Spirit also helpeth our for we know not what we should pra